Life is Good!

lessons in joyful living

LIFE IS GOOD!
LESSONS IN JOYFUL LIVING
is published by

YORKVILLE PRESS
NEW YORK, NEW YORK

Library of Congress Cataloging-in-Publication Data
is on file with the publisher.

PHOTOGRAPHY BY: *Monique Stauder*
DESIGN AND PRODUCTION BY: *Tina Taylor*

ISBN 0-9729427-7-7
Printed in Canada by Friesens

jes 10 9 8 7 6 5 4 3 2 1

Life is Good!

lessons in joyful living

by trixie koontz, dog
edited by dean koontz

CANINE COMPANIONS FOR INDEPENDENCE

Trixie, a former service dog for the wheelchair bound, retired at three with an elbow problem, and came to live with the Koontz family. She is donating all author royalties from this book to **Canine Companions for Independence,** the wonderful organization that originally raised and trained her.

*I, Trixie (who is dog), dedicate this book to Dr. Wayne Berry,
who is best veterinary neurosurgeon in the known world and
also very kind. Because of Dr. Berry's excellent spinal surgery,
I run, swim, and play again.*

*I, Trixie (who is still dog), also dedicate this book to my
wonderful vets, Dr. Bill Lyle and Dr. Bruce Whitaker.
All dogs should be so lucky to have caring doctors like them.*

Contents

INTRODUCTION

smell sausages! gonna get sausages!

I Trixie Koontz (who is dog) am happy twenty-four hours, fifty-eight minutes, and thirty seconds every day. Am unhappy only for thirty seconds after breakfast, after lunch, and after dinner because food gone, leaving empty dish. Empty dish looks as deep as eternity. Eternity reminds me no one lives forever. Remembering no one lives forever, I am sad. So sad. Tail won't wag. Try again. Won't wag. Try again. Nada. Have desire to read French novels about futility of life. Then remember next meal—or snack—comes in four hours. Tail wags. Wags all by itself. Day grows brighter. Realize dish must be empty before it can be filled again. Empty dish is promise of full dish to come. Life is good. Time to pee.

While peeing, realize most humans are unhappy more than one and half minutes per day. Could help humanity by writing book, sharing dog philosophy of joyful living. Am scared about writing. Can type with pencil in mouth, but am scared of semicolons. Don't understand purpose of semicolons. Stupid, stupid, stupid semicolons. Must write entire book without semicolons. And use exclamation points sparingly. Am dog (me, Trixie) so have tendency to get excited! Must not get excited! Must not use lots of ! exclamation points ! because will look like silly puppy and will be laughed at by cats who never ! use exclamation points ! because they think they are *sooooo* cool!!!!

Writing is hard. Must give up important ball chasing, important napping, important sniffing to write. Work hard. So many words. Hate stupid semicolons. Hate; hate; hate. Chew up pencils in frustration.

Finish book. Give to dad (Dean Koontz, who is human). Then I rip guts out of duck. Duck is not real, is Booda duck, stuffed toy. I am gentle dog. Cannot hurt real duck or even mean stupid ugly crazy cat. But am demon with stuffed toys. Work off tension. Rip, rip, rip. Feel pretty good. Cough up soggy wad of Booda-duck stuffing. Feel even better.

Here is book for you. How to live more joyfully. Get yourself stuffed Booda duck. Squeak it with teeth. Rip, rip, rip. You'll feel better. I, Trixie (who is dog), got lots more where that one came from.

Trixie

ABOUT THE AUTHOR

My nose.
Big, black, beautiful, cold, wet.
Every day, remember to love your
nose. It does nice things for you.

My big eyes, long lashes.
Use to get extra treats. You try
same trick. Someone might even
give you peanut butter on spoon.
Or new Cadillac.

My big teeth, long tongue.
Teeth scare cats. Maybe not your
teeth, but use 'em to smile. Tongue
is for tasting and for wiping nose.
Maybe your tongue not long enough
to wipe nose. Better carry hanky.

My big padded paws.
Webbed toes for swimming. Dad
says I have prettier paws than
most authors. Prettier than John
Grisham's. Maybe even prettier
than Anne Tyler's paws.

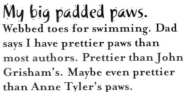

11

Dog naps are cool!

Cat naps way too short. Can work much better after nice long dog nap!

The poet Homer (not a dog) wrote "Sleep is the twin of death." Get me a blue doodoo bag. That Homer stuff is a pile of poop. Sleep is just life slowed down. So you can rest. So you can dream about bacon. And chicken. And sausage. And cantaloupe. And peanut butter. And about buying a fancy convertible and driving around the USA, pee-marking territory till it's all *mine*.

To live joyfully, learn to love sleep. Love naps. Love snoozing with eyes open, fool boss. Sleep is not like death. Dumb Homer. After death, is no sleep, just fun and food and play and adventure and driving fast cars. Sleep is blessing of this world only.

When not napping, buy hard red-rubber bone to chew on. It soothes nerves at work. Better than getting in nervous snit, chewing on boss, fellow workers, loved ones. Never chew on people. You are not crocodile. Neither am I, Trixie, who is dog. Do I look like crocodile? No. If you look in mirror and see crocodile, get plastic surgery. Red-rubber bone will not be enough to soothe you.

13

Water is restful. Swim in water. Play in water. Never pee in water. Only fish pee in water. Fish have excuse, are never out of water and are very dumb. No offense to fish, but is true. No fish ever wrote book like this. Lassie saved Timmy every time he fall down well. No fish ever saved Timmy or ever could. Have nothing against fish. Are very tasty, go good with chips. Don't like sharks. Sharks mean, dangerous, make one good movie and then hundreds bad boring movies, should be ashamed of themselves. Same is true of dinosaurs. Glad I didn't live in age of dinosaurs. No blue bags big enough to keep Jurrasic era clean.

In pool is fun to play with ball. Or in yard. Or in park. Or in living room. Dad taught me game—he holds hollow rubber ball under water, lets go, ball pops into air, I snatch it in teeth. Learned to lie on float, hold ball under water with my own paws, play game myself. Mom and Dad say, "Smart dog, so smart." Is true, I guess. Smarter than dinosaurs, who couldn't teach themselves games and got extinct. Playing games is fun, makes life good. Play and be joyful. Be careful if play games like poker, craps, and blackjack. Could loose treat money. All those hotels in Vegas built with lost treat money, leaving dogs without cookies. Bad Vegas.

Playing games is fun, makes life good. Play and be joyful. Happy dog! 15

Life is Good!

Life is good! Life is good! Life is good! Life is good! Life is good! Life is good! Life is good! Life is good! Life is good! Life is good! Life is good! Life is good! Life is good! Life is good! Life is good! Life is good! Life is good! Life is good! Life is good! Life is good!

Always take time to smell the flowers and laugh til'

ZZZZZZZZZZZZZZZZZzzzz

MOONLIGHT THEATER

Life is good if you go to movies.

Popcorn. Soft pretzels. Hot dogs. Roasted chicken breast with mashed potatoes and gravy (in dream theaters). Me, Trixie, who is dog (good dog, good), loves movies. Last week saw *King Kong*, saw *The Thin Man*, really liked *The Big Sleep*. Warning! Don't go see *Old Yeller*! Ending sucks! *Old Yeller* written by angry hateful crazy cat! Or Satan!

In Thin Man movies is smart dog named Asta. Like all dogs, Asta is funny. All dogs except Old Yeller—and Lassie, so busy saving stupid Timmy, she never had time to be funny. And did Timmy ever give her peanut butter? No. Mostly, he just said, "Thanks, girl," and ran straight off into burning barn or quicksand.

Like Lassie, all dogs are easy. That's one secret to joyful living. If you don't expect too much of people, won't be disappointed. Might be surprised by treat. Disappointment is bad. Surprise treats are good. Sometimes unconditional love comes back to you. If it doesn't, you still feel good 'cause you gave it. That was deep thought. Dogs have 'em all the time. Don't usually tell people our deep thoughts 'cause don't want to be boring. You want boring, get parrot. Get ant farm. Ants and parrots never star in movies. Except cartoon parrots and giant radioactive ants. Old Yeller should have been giant radioactive ant instead of dog like me, who is Trixie. Would be better movie.

21

Joyful living means think of

yourself as movie star.

But don't act like one. Not like bad one, anyway. Don't get drunk, punch photographer. Don't get drunk, punch fan. Don't get drunk, punch reporter. Get drunk, just punch self. Don't throw hissy fit about size of location trailer. Don't get married five times in one year. Don't get caught naked in public unless have fur like dog. Don't go on TV talk show, whine about price of fame, look like idiot. Be good movie star, work for dog charities, never star in crazy-sick movie like *Old Yeller*. Remember, not everyone in movie is star. There are supporting roles. They can be pretty, too. And smart. And happy. There's got to be character actors and walk-ons. They aren't shot at, beaten up, and chased by dinosaurs as much as stars.

Be proud but not arrogant. Be beautiful but not vain. Be strong but gentle. Be loving, be humble, be as much like a dog as you can— and be happy!

23

Find work that makes you happy

Get to work on time. Put down your bone toy.

PONDER ETERNAL MYSTERIES
Like...did Shakespeare really write plays himself or did his dog help?

and life will be good.

Be concise

Think twice

Think thrice

Be nice

Concentrate

Collaborate

Confer

Concur

Brood

Conclude

Agree

Go pee?

25

Accomplishment

Dad gives editorial suggestions. Stupid, stupid, stupid editorial suggestions. He is not editor. Is writer. Like me. I pretend to listen. Am actually thinking about bacon. Bacon is good. Bacon is very good. I am good, too. People call me "good dog, good, very good." Bacon is very good. I am very good. But I am not bacon. Why not? Mysterious. Am being bad dog. At work, should not daydream. Work is for gossiping with fellow workers and wasting time on Internet. Don't have any fellow workers but Dad and Mom. Don't have own Internet access. Have no choice but keep paw to page. Page is finished. Good? Bad? Cannot be sure until taste. Ummmm. Not as good as bacon. But better than last three bestsellers I read. Work done is accomplishment. Accomplishment is happiness. Happiness is red-rubber bone.

is happiness.

27

Chase! Chase! Chase! Chase! Chase! Chase! Chase! Chase! Chase! C

Summer!

Summer is for running in grass. Summer is for splashing in surf. Chase ball! Chase butterfly! Chase cat! Go to vet for treatment of nose scratches. Chase Frisbee! Chase Mom! Chase Dad! Chase cat! Vet again. Chase ball! Chase tail! Begin to notice sameness in leisure-time activities. Pull tug-toy snake. Pull tug-toy bone. Pull, pull, pull! Pull tug-toy rope. Swim. Lie on float in pool. Splash! Blow bubbles through nose! Blow bubbles through other end! OUT OF THE POOL, BAD DOG, BAD DOG! Wriggle in summer grass. Get belly rub from Mom. Get belly rub from dad. Get belly rub from Aunt Linda. Get belly rub from Aunt Elaine. Linda. Elaine. Linda. Elaine. Dad. Mom. Belly rub, belly rub, belly rub, belly rub! Read *Bleak House* by Charles Dickens, study brilliant characterizations, ponder the tragedy of the human condition. New tennis ball! Chase! Chase! Chase, chase, chase! Suddenly is September.

Chase! Chase! Chase! Chase! Chase! Chase! Chase

Grass. Lose job, wreck car, endure tornado…nothing matters if you have lawn or meadow. Lie in grass. Smell grass. Sneeze. Listen to breeze in grass. Sneeze. Sigh.

Sighhhhhhhhhhhhhhhhhhhhhhhh

Life is Good!

Life is long path. Is
lonely to walk it only
with your shadow. Walk
with friends, with family.
Walk even with cat if you
have to. Share your heart,
and lonely path becomes
happy parade. Sounds like
cheesy greeting card, but is true.
Which reminds me: cheese. Don't
just stop along path to smell roses.
Stop for cheese sometimes. More
cheese than roses. No bees in cheese.
Path of life has walls and fences. People
build them around you. You build most
yourself. Look through fences, see what's
on other side. You make your own path.
Sounds like greeting-card baloney but is true.
Which reminds me: baloney, frankfurters, thinly
sliced deli chicken breast. Don't hurry. The more
stops along the path, the tastier your life.

Share your heart,
and lonely path becomes happy parade.

Life is Good!

Allow yourself to daydream.

Daydreams can come true. I daydreamed about dangle ball. Got one. I daydreamed about cookies. Got some. I daydreamed about watermelon. Got some. I daydream big rig loaded with frankfurters overturns in street in front of house, nobody hurt, but 20,000 weenies scatter across pavement, and I'm only dog for miles around, and same day Mom buys 20-gallon drum of mustard at Costco. Hasn't happened yet, but Mom just bought some mustard, so truck will overturn soon. **Daydreams can come true.**

Life is good when you

believe you are beautiful.

Everyone is beautiful somehow, some way. Some need bows. Some are beautiful without 'em. Some have beautiful voices, some beautiful minds. Some are beautiful like sunsets, some beautiful like cheese. Some have fur and tails, and are adored. Be a sunset, be cheese, be furry, be whatever beautiful you are, and beautiful things will come to you along the path of life. The only ugly puss is a sourpuss. Dog wisdom.

37

Smack your lips loud!

Be thankful for your bowls. Good things come in them. Sometimes water. Sometimes juice. Sometimes kibble. Sometimes cantaloupe. Always show thanks for what's in bowls. Smack your lips loud. Lick chops. Drool. Drooling is best way to say thank-you. Can't fake drool. Humans would be happier if drooled more. More drool equals nicer world. Nicer, wetter, stickier. Wear rubber-soled shoes, stain-resistant fabrics. Drool, be happy.

PONDER ETERNAL MYSTERIES
Like…when cow jumped over moon, how could dish run away with spoon when neither have legs?

Life is Good!

39

Never miss a chance to share laughs with those you love.
Life will give you enough time to share tears.

Loving nature makes joyful life. Mother Nature
made me, made you. Also made scorpions, cockroaches. Mother
Nature is little nuts but very creative. Mother Nature gives warm
sun, cool rain, pretty ferns. She gives tornadoes, hurricanes.
Mother Nature is like wacky aunt from Cleveland, comes visiting
with nice gifts, also eye-watering garlic breath and killer farts,
but is family, so you got to love her.

PONDER ETERNAL MYSTERIES
Like…after watching cat cough up hairball, why would anyone want cat?

Howl a little. Let loose.

Say "I am here." Say "I am dog," or whatever it is you are. Don't howl "I am dog," if you are not dog. You'll look stupid.

HAVE A GOOD NOSE FOR HOLIDAYS

Celebrate every chance you get. Thanksgiving is my favorite. Have good Thanksgiving memories. Turkey. Turkey, turkey, turkey! Pumpkin pie! Yams. Yams stick to roof of mouth. Don't like yams. Yams taste like bad cat. Ha, ha, ha. Never really ate cat. Am good dog, good.  Turkey, turkey! Chestnut filling. Mashed potatoes. Graaaaavy! Gravy and turkey—bliss. Gravy and mashed potatoes—to die for. Gravy and pumpkin pie—mistake. Gravy and chestnut filling—delicious. Tried gravy and cat. Cat became very angry. Ha, ha, ha. Joke.

My first Thanksgiving memory is landing on Plymouth Rock with pilgrims. That was in other life. I was goat. Sailed from England, butted lots of Pilgrims overboard for fun. They wanted to eat me for Thanksgiving. But Indians brought corn and turkey and Hostess cupcakes. When I was goat, owed my life to Indians.

I remember Thanksgiving 1878. Was cow-herding dog in Old West. Liked cows. Much in common with cows. Cows don't like yams. Cows think cats stupid. My master had no turkey that year. Only cows. I could not eat my friends, the cows. In dark of night, set loose all cows. "Run, dear cows!" I whispered. "Run, run for your lives, dear cows! Be free like cats and yams and other things that taste too bad to eat!" Next Thanksgiving I remember is 1916, I am cat. This is Reincarnation We Don't Talk About.

To be happy, use your nose. Every day is rich in smells.

Life is Good!

Bacon...

Skunk...

Dad...

Mom...

Doughnuts...

Cookies...
in jar, in cupboard.
Where I can't get at 'em...

48

...a cliché, sure, but if you got roses,

smell 'em.

NEW YEAR'S RESOLUTIONS

Life will be joyful if you improve yourself. Me too. Even dog can use improvement. I, Trixie (who is dog), resolve each New Year's Eve to be better dog in all ways starting 12:00:01 a.m., but not one second sooner. Am told all the time by Mom, by Dad that I am good dog, good dog. Don't know how could be better. But would like to be told am perfect dog, perfect, 'cause maybe perfect dog gets more treats than good. So, my resolutions:

3 recommend all Dad's books at next Mensa meeting

1 be furrier

5 avoid say nice things about cats immediately after eat frankfurters

2 wag tail more

4 say nice things about cats even if every time say nice things will vomit

6 get own newspaper subscription so don't have to read Dad's and get drool on food pages before he reads 'em

7 find out if other book writers besides Dad live in neighborhood, then pee on their lawns

8 register and vote like good citizen

9 pick up after myself with blue bags

10 put blue bags in garbage instead of in Dad's shoes, no matter how funny would be in shoes

Books make life good!

Books are fun. Dad's books are especially fun. (I know where my kibble comes from.) Some books confuse me. Read *War and Peace* by Tolstoy. Long book. Very long book. No dogs in significant roles. Why anyone write very long book not about dogs? Figured I read bad translation. Read it again in original Russian language. Still no dogs. Tolstoy was maniac, writing very long books not about dogs. *War and Peace* gets a no-cookie rating from this critic. Plus I peed on book. Critic is entitled to strong opinion.

Read Dad's new book. Can give honest opinion even though I know who scoops my kibble. Am dog, after all. Am incorruptible.

Dad's new book is suspenseful, funny, full of emotion, but has no dog in significant role. Am afraid Dad is losing mind. Will end up as nuts as Tolstoy though not as Russian.

Your life is an epic novel. Dare to be the hero

at the center of your story.

A joyful life needs to have purpose.

Maybe purpose is healing sick.
Maybe is helping poor. Maybe
is making people laugh. Maybe
purpose is chasing ball on water,
on land, wherever is thrown,
chase, chase, chase! You may
not be Olympic star. Me neither.
But chasing makes heart strong,
the better to love with.

54

Meditate.

Meditation is calming

I, Trixie, am meditating dog. I meditate on green dangle ball. So many mysteries to ponder. Where do dangle balls come from? Do always just appear on floor one day like mine did? Why urge to shake heck out of dangle ball every time I see it? Why green? Who is really in control: me or dangle ball? Only time I ever growl is while shaking dangle ball...so does dangle ball have unholy appeal to my dark side? Is dangle ball made by *Satan*?

Sometimes when meditating, I appear to be asleep. Dogs don't sleep much. Mostly meditate, think deep thoughts. Here I meditate about how nice and warm is sunshine.

Here I meditate about sleep.

Life is better

58

Toys can be simple like rainbow snake with two squeaking heads or bigger like 400-foot yacht with swimming pool and movie theater...Excuse me while I wipe my nose and think about yacht for a minute. Yacht or snake...yacht or snake... Snake is definitely more fun. Bite yacht, it doesn't squeak.

Life is Good!

with toys.

Wriggle every chance you get. Ahhhh

Life is Good!

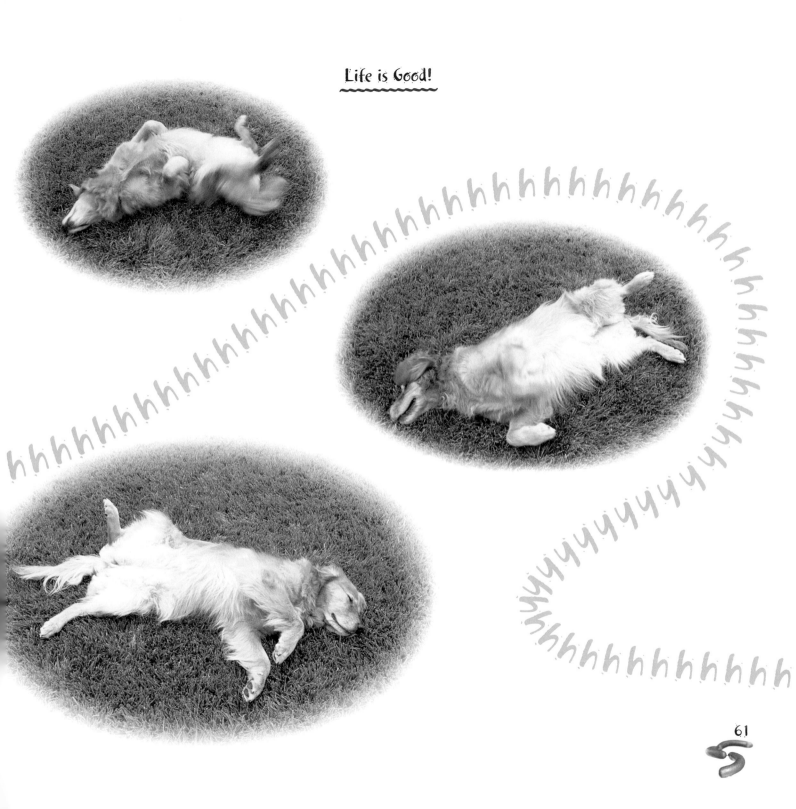

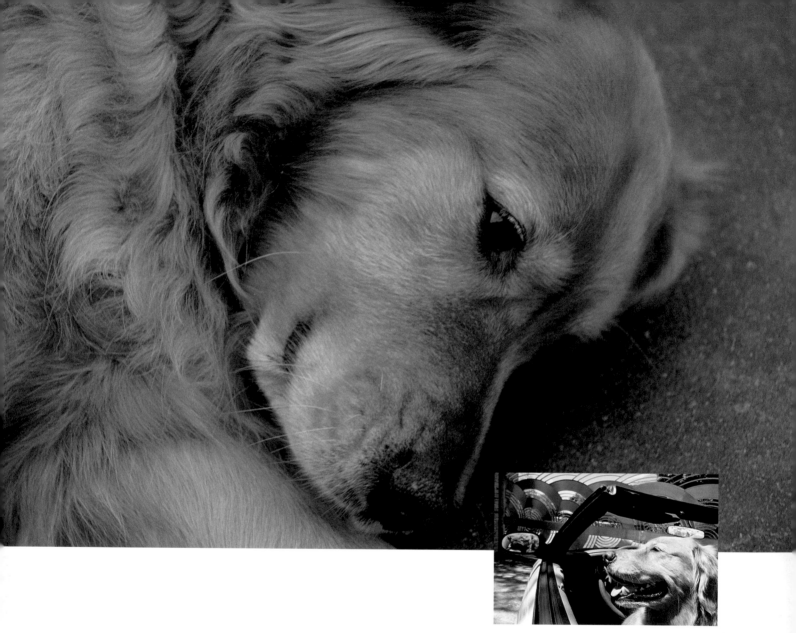

How good it would be to take Mom's car. Drive to beach. Drive to Farmer John sausage factory. Drive to ice-cream shop. Wheels are freedom. Know what bigger freedom is? Imagination. In mind, dogs can drive. In mind, we are always free.

TRIXIE'S TOP 8 REASONS
WHY DOGS SHOULD BE ALLOWED TO DRIVE CARS

1. We are by nature obedient. Would break no traffic laws. Except when toilet stops require brief parking in front of fireplugs.

2. Look so cute. Sight of driving dog lift spirits of human drivers, make highways friendlier.

3. Because ears tend to flap in wind, dogs make better use of convertibles than humans do.

4. Dogs do not drink alcoholic beverages. So can never drive under influence and never blast passengers with beer farts.

5. Guide dogs who drive could better serve blind people.

6. Is civil-rights issue.

7. Have better self-image, bark less, wag more.

8. Dogs don't need maps. Can smell our way anywhere.

63

Let mystery be key to open heart and mind.

Mystery.

Life is full of mystery. Think about mystery.

Let mystery be key to open heart and mind. Wonder will come in. Wonder brings happiness.

Fern shadows on wall look real. Want to bite. Can't. Shadows are real but made of nothing. Can't be touched. Can't be tasted. Wind is real, can be felt, can be heard, but can't be seen.

Dogs are real. So is invisible part of us that, when we die, goes to a meadow this side of Rainbow Bridge and waits for those we love. When you come to us, we wag and dance and kiss—and cross the bridge with you to What Comes Next.

Eat joyfully! Can't live on kibble
alone. Must have treats. Mom spreads little apricot jelly
on rice cake, gives me pieces with jelly side down, so
tongue gets full taste. Have your mom or dad give you
jelly-side-down treats, and life will be good. If you have
hands, you can even give treats to yourself. Would almost
give up tail for hands…except would look funny with
hands where tail used to be.

Peanut butter.

Butter made of peanuts. No cows involved. Cows get day off when peanut butter made. More than anything else, peanut butter explains why humans rule world, dogs don't. Give yourself spoon of peanut butter now and then. You'll be happier. Cows, too.

67

ANOTHER HOLIDAY!

Holidays make life joyful.
I, Trixie (born dog and still dog), love Halloween. Dress up like witch. Tour neighborhood. Fill bag with goodies. Return home. Dress up like Frankenpuppy. Tour neighborhood. Fill second bag with goodies. Return home. Dress up like terrifying extraterrestrial. Tour neighborhood, demand goodies or will liquify with ray gun. Return home with lots of goodies. Insert in mouth giant wax fangs, spray whipped cream on muzzle to fake rabies, chase neighborhood children who are trick-or-treating, terrify into dropping their bags of goodies. Snatch bags. Return home. Pee. Dress up like Lassie, go to bakery, convince everyone Timmy is trapped under overturned tanker truck. Get everyone to leave bakery to help Timmy. I loot store. Experience moment of guilt. Chastise self: "Bad dog. Bad dog. Bad, bad dog." Go to butcher shop. Convince everyone Timmy is trapped in burning sawmill. Get everyone to leave butcher shop to help Timmy. Grab all frankfurters and steaks. Experience moment of guilt. Decide can live with it. Go home. Eat. Eat, eat, eat. Throw up. Write memoir of criminal activities. Sell to major publisher. Sell film rights to Steven Spielberg. Go on book and movie tour. Stay in 4-star hotels with room service. Order six dozen all-beef frankfurters every night. Go to Betty Ford clinic to take cure for serious frankfurter addiction. Do spot on Dr. Phil's show. Weep. Win audience sympathy. Sneak into Dr. Phil's dressing room, get his American Express card number, order one million frankfurters. Take vacation in Tahiti. Plan for next Halloween.

As for that Halloween story.... Wink, wink. Nudge, nudge.

Don't struggle against life.

You get no philosophy with this picture. It's here just 'cause Mom and Dad think I have cute furry butt. Parents. Embarrassing.

Float with it. Be Bouyant.
You won't sink unless you expect to.

The dog's eye
sees to the heart of truth:
the purpose of life is love.

Play hard. Play, play, play like your life depends on it. Because it does.

PONDER ETERNAL MYSTERIES
Like…who let the dog out? Who? Who? Who-who?

To lead good life, must have curiosity…

even if sometimes the mystery in the bushes turns out to be skunk.

75

Always aspire to great heights.

Here, with three paws off the ground, I am only
one paw away from being bird. I *know* I can fly!

Accept affection.

Encourage affection.
Position yourself in hallway
or other high-traffic area.
As giver-of-affection
approaches, look cute,
reach out with one paw,
and then roll onto back
with all four paws in the air,
offering glorious furry belly
for rubbing. If you don't
have glorious furry belly,
this might not work as well
for you as does for me.

77

THE DARK SIDE

Life is good, good life, good. But sometimes has dark side. Must be aware of dark side but not over-whelmed by it. Must laugh at dark side. Ha-ha-ha to hurricanes. Ha-ha-ha to giant asteroid maybe going to collide with Earth. Here are some bad things I, Trixie, who is laughing dog, say ha-ha-ha to:

1. Say ha-ha-ha to dog-catcher. Have, license, am on leash. He can't touch me. Live by rules. Some-times feel stifled but am untouchable.

2. Say ha-ha-ha to mountain lions live in nearby canyon and want to eat dogs. Say ha-ha-ha from behind tall fence they can't climb.

3. Say ha-ha-ha to fleas and ticks. Am on program, have no fleas and ticks. Have only spider named Fred. Keep Fred in jar. Feed him flies. As pet, Fred is as much fun as fungus.

4. Say ha-ha-ha to bees. Snap at one bothering me. Get stung. Say ha-ha-ha . Face swells, look weird. Say ha-ha-ha. Have to go to vet, get injection of Benadryl. Say ha-ha-ha , but now people look at me funny, like maybe laughter has crazy edge.

5. Never say ha-ha-ha to mailman who HAS COME TO KILL US ALL. Instead of ha-ha-ha, hide behind sofa, hope for survival.

6. Say ha-ha-ha when stupid judges at Westminster Dog Show pick best of show that isn't golden retriever. Say ha-ha-ha , send stern letter.

7. Say ha-ha-ha to thunder. Dad says thunder only God bowling. Of course Dad also say mailman NOT come to kill us all. Sometimes Dad is so naive.

8. Say ha-ha-ha to hunting coyote packs howling in dead of night. Say ha-ha-ha, then jump in bed with Mom and Dad.

9. Say ha-ha-ha to grinning Halloween pumpkin with fire in eyes. Say ha-ha-ha but back away careful. Go to market. Buy pumpkin pie. Eat pie in front of grinning pumpkin with fiery eyes. Show who is boss.

10. Say ha-ha-ha when Mom and Dad watch scary movies. Say ha-ha-ha and hide head under sofa pillows. If you can't see monster, then monster can't see you.

Lie on back in grass.
Wave at sky with hind foot.
Maybe God will give belly rub.